Phillip Reynolds

AGE 10-11
Key Stage 2

national TESTS **practice papers**
FOR THE YEAR 2002

Key Stage 2
Mental Arithmetic Book 2

Contents	Page
Introduction	
The National Tests: A Summary	iii
Mental Maths at Key Stage 2	iv
Mental Maths Tests	
Question Pages	1
Answer Sheets	13
Answers	25
National Curriculum Levels	28
Practice Pages	
Questions	29
Answers	42

First published 2001
exclusively for WHSmith by

Hodder & Stoughton Educational,
a division of Hodder Headline Ltd
338 Euston Road
London NW1 3BH

Text © Hodder & Stoughton Educational 2001

All rights reserved. No part of this publication may be reproduced or transmitted in any form or by any means, electronic or mechanical, including photocopying, recording or any information storage and retrieval system, without permission in writing from the publisher.

A CIP record for this book is available from the British Library.

Authors: Steve Mills and Hilary Koll

ISBN 0340 84602 X

Printed and bound by Graphycems, Spain

NOTE: The tests, questions and advice in this book are not reproductions of the official test materials sent to schools. The official testing process is supported by guidance and training for teachers in setting and marking tests and interpreting the results. The results achieved in the tests in this book may not be the same as are achieved in the official tests.

Introduction

The National Tests: A Summary

What are the National Tests?

Children who attend state schools in England and Wales sit National Tests (SATs) at the ages of 7, 11 and 14, usually at the beginning of May. They may also sit optional tests in the intervening years – many schools have chosen to adopt these tests. The test results are accompanied by an assessment by the child's teacher.

The results are used by the school to assess each child's level of knowledge and progress in English and Maths at Key Stage 1 and English, Maths and Science at Key Stages 2 and 3. They also provide useful guidance for the child's next teacher.

The educational calendar for children aged 5-14 is structured as follows:

Key Stage	Year	Age by end of year	National Test
1 (KS1)	1	6	
	2	7	KEY STAGE 1
2 (KS2)	3	8	Optional Year 3
	4	9	Optional Year 4
	5	10	Optional Year 5
	6	11	KEY STAGE 2
3 (KS3)	7	12	
	8	13	
	9	14	KEY STAGE 3

Test Timetable

The Key Stage 1 National Tests are carried out in **May**.

Key Stage 2 tests take place in one week in May. All children sit the same test at the same time. In 2002, the tests will take place in the week of **13–17 May**. Your child's school will be able to provide you with a detailed timetable.

Key Stage 3 students will sit their tests on **7–13 May**.

Levels

National average levels have been set for children's results in the National Tests. The levels are as follows:

LEVEL	AGE 7	AGE 11	AGE 14
8			
7			
6			
5			
4			
3			
2			
2a			
2b			
2c			
1			

- Below expected level
- Expected level
- Above expected level
- Exceptional

Results

Your child's school will send you a report indicating his or her levels in the tests and the teacher assessment.

The school's overall test results will be included in local and national league tables, which are published in most newspapers.

What can parents do to help?

While it is never a good idea to encourage cramming, you can help your child to succeed by:

- Making sure he or she has enough food, sleep and leisure time during the test period.
- Practising important skills such as writing and reading stories, spelling and mental arithmetic.
- Telling him or her what to expect in the test, such as important symbols and key words.
- Helping him or her to be comfortable in test conditions including working within a time limit, reading questions carefully and understanding different ways of answering.

Introduction

Mental Maths at Key Stage 2

Most children at Key Stage 2 will take an orally delivered Mental Maths Test and two written tests. This book contains 12 Mental Maths Tests and practice questions for the range of topics covered.

The marks given to each child in the national Mental Maths Test are used in conjunction with the marks gained in the written tests to find out a National Curriculum level, with a typical 11-year-old attaining Level 4.

To gain an idea of the level at which your child is working, use the table on page 28, which shows you how to convert your child's marks for each Mental Maths Test into a National Curriculum level. Children working at the expected level or above should aim to score more than 11 marks out of 20 in each test.

Setting the tests

Do not expect your child to take the tests one after another. Taking the tests regularly over a few weeks can provide your child with sufficient practice and can help him or her to notice improvements and to track progress.

Your child will only need a pencil and rubber for each test.

Each mental test should take approximately 10-15 minutes to give. It consists of:

- A list of twenty questions to be read aloud – cut this out for ease of use.
- An answer sheet that your child should use for recording answers.

Read each question twice and allow only the time suggested for your child to answer.

Questions in the national Mental Maths Test cover a wider range than just calculation in your head. Where mental calculation is required, your child can make small jottings on the answer sheets to help him or her retain information from the question. These must then NOT be used to form the basis of written calculations: children are not allowed to 'work out' answers on paper. For example, if a question asks children to multiply 25 by 8, your child could jot down 25 and 8, but cannot then set it out as a written multiplication question to find the answer. Instead a mental method should be used, such as using a 'double, double, double' method for multiplying by 8, i.e. 25…50…100…200.

Marking the tests

Discuss the answers with your child and encourage him or her to explain the methods used to reach an answer. Any mental method that reaches the correct answer should be praised, although alternative and perhaps quicker methods can be discussed.

Keep a record of your child's scores for each test to monitor his or her progress.

Test 1
Questions

"For this first set of questions you have five seconds to work out each answer and write it down."

1. What is the product of nine and eight?
2. Write the number twelve thousand and five in figures.
3. Subtract forty from one hundred and ten.
4. How many millilitres are there in one point two litres?
5. Decrease three thousand by two.
6. What is ninety per cent as a decimal?

"For the next set of questions you have ten seconds to work out each answer and write it down."

7. A number lies between thirty and forty. When it is divided by ten there is a remainder of three. What is the number?
8. The temperature yesterday was minus seven degrees Celsius. The temperature today is four degrees warmer. What is the temperature today?
9. Look at the answer sheet. In the equation, what is the value of x?
10. What time is exactly forty minutes after half past six in the morning? Give your answer in digital form.
11. What is one third of nine point six?
12. Two numbers have a difference of one point four. One number is six point eight. What could the other number be?
13. Look at the answer sheet. Circle the number that is nearest to two thirds.
14. Sandeep slept for nine and a quarter hours without waking. He went to sleep at nine fifteen p.m. What time did he wake?
15. Look at the answer sheet. What is the median of the numbers?

"For the next set of questions you have fifteen seconds to work out each answer and write it down."

16. Look at the answer sheet. Draw a ring around the number that is a multiple of nine.
17. A regular shape has a perimeter of forty two centimetres. Each side is seven centimetres. What is the name of the shape?
18. I have thirty pence. My friend has five times that much. How much do we have altogether?
19. Which number is exactly half way between three thousand six hundred and four thousand?
20. Look at the answer sheet. What is the size of angle G?

Test 2
Questions

"For this first set of questions you have five seconds to work out each answer and write it down."

1. Add sixty eight and twenty one.
2. How many grams are there in one quarter of a kilogram?
3. Multiply eighteen by ten.
4. Write the decimal that is equivalent to nine tenths.
5. Divide forty five by nine.
6. How many twenty pence pieces have the same value as two pounds?

"For the next set of questions you have ten seconds to work out each answer and write it down."

7. Add three point six and two point six.
8. Double two hundred and seventy.
9. A girl buys a sixty five pence magazine. She pays with a five pound note. How much change is she given?
10. A bag contains three red balls and two yellow balls. The probability of picking a red ball is three fifths. What is the probability of picking a yellow ball?
11. A coat costs twenty pounds. In a sale the shop reduces all prices by twenty per cent. How much does the coat cost in the sale?
12. Look at the answer sheet. How many lines of reflective symmetry does the regular pentagon have?
13. Imagine a square based pyramid. How many vertices does it have?
14. A full bag of sugar weighs one kilogram. How many grams will it weigh when it is one quarter full?
15. In a class there are three boys to every girl. How many are girls if there are 40 children altogether in the class?

"For the next set of questions you have fifteen seconds to work out each answer and write it down."

16. One side of a square is three point two centimetres. What is the perimeter of the square?
17. Two numbers have a difference of one point nine. The higher number is eleven point one. What is the lower number?
18. There are three times as many children as adults at a funfair. There are exactly one hundred and eight people at the fair. How many are adults?
19. Which year was thirteen years before the year two thousand and two?
20. Which number on your answer sheet is an approximate answer to the question 'What is seventeen percent of ninety nine?'

Test 3
Questions

"For this first set of questions you have five seconds to work out each answer and write it down."

1. What is seven multiplied by three?
2. How many months are there in two years?
3. Write the number eleven thousand and fourteen in figures.
4. How many grams are there in one point five kilograms?
5. What is three tenths as a decimal?
6. What number is four less than five thousand?

"For the next set of questions you have ten seconds to work out each answer and write it down."

7. A pen costs seventy pence and a pencil case costs one pound ninety nine pence. How much do the pen and pencil case cost altogether?
8. The temperature yesterday was two degrees Celsius. The temperature today is eight degrees colder. What is the temperature today?
9. Look at the answer sheet. In the equation, what is the value of n?
10. What is one tenth of eighty six?
11. Multiply seven by twenty five.
12. Two numbers have a total of fifty. One number is seventeen. What is the other number?
13. Look at the answer sheet. Circle the number that is nearest to ten metres.
14. Molly slept for nine and a half hours without waking. She went to sleep at ten p.m. What time did she wake?
15. Look at the answer sheet. What is the mean of the three test scores?

"For the next set of questions you have fifteen seconds to work out each answer and write it down."

16. Look at the answer sheet. Draw a ring around the smallest of the five numbers.
17. A regular shape has a perimeter of thirty six centimetres. Each side is nine centimetres. What is the name of the shape?
18. I have ninety pence. My friend has four times that much. How much do we have altogether?
19. Which number is exactly half way between two thousand and five thousand?
20. Look at the answer sheet. What is the size of angle B?

Test 4

Questions

"For this first set of questions you have five seconds to work out each answer and write it down."

1. What is four multiplied by eleven?
2. How many days are there in five weeks?
3. Write the number ten thousand and three in figures.
4. How many millilitres are there in a quarter of a litre?
5. What is nought point seven as a fraction?
6. What is sixty multiplied by four?

"For the next set of questions you have ten seconds to work out each answer and write it down."

7. How many minutes are there in ten hours?
8. Add sixteen to fourteen and then multiply by five.
9. Look at the answer sheet. In the equation, what is the value of n?
10. One third of a number is nine. What is the number?
11. Divide one thousand by one hundred.
12. The time is quarter past ten in the evening. Write this as it would be shown on a twenty-four hour digital clock.
13. Look at the answer sheet. Draw a ring around the decimal that is equivalent to ninety per cent.
14. Sam's maths lesson started at five to nine in the morning. It lasted one hour. What time did the lesson end? Write your answer in digital form.
15. Look at the answer sheet. What is the mode of these numbers?

"For the next set of questions you have fifteen seconds to work out each answer and write it down."

16. Look at the answer sheet. Draw a ring around the number nearest to one.
17. A rectangle has sides of two point six centimetres and three point four centimetres. What is its perimeter?
18. Imagine a circle. If a straight cut was made through the centre of the circle to form two identical shapes, what would these shapes be called?
19. Look at the answer sheet. Draw a ring around any of the numbers that are square numbers.
20. Look at the answer sheet. It takes thirty eight minutes to get from the shopping centre to the cinema. Write what time the bus arrives at the cinema.

Test 5
Questions

"For this first set of questions you have five seconds to work out each answer and write it down."

1. Write the number forty thousand and sixteen in figures.
2. What is thirty three more than fifteen?
3. What is sixty seven divided by ten?
4. What is two thirds of nine?
5. How many degrees are there in one of the angles of an equilateral triangle?
6. How many weeks are there in two years?

"For the next set of questions you have ten seconds to work out each answer and write it down."

7. Add twelve and eighteen and then divide by six.
8. What is half of five point two?
9. Two lengths add to make one metre. One of the lengths is seventeen centimetres. What is the other length?
10. A cartoon programme lasts for twenty minutes. It starts at ten minutes to five. What time does it end?
11. A shop has fifty per cent off all prices. What is the new price of a book that was thirteen pounds?
12. On the answer sheet is part of a scale. What number is the arrow pointing to?
13. Imagine a square based pyramid. How many of its faces are rectangles?
14. A one litre jug is half full. How many more millilitres are needed to fill it?
15. A football team scored five goals for every two they let in. They scored fifteen goals. How many did they let in?

"For the next set of questions you have fifteen seconds to work out each answer and write it down."

16. Which number is exactly half way between thirty four and forty four?
17. Find the total of twenty two, thirty three and forty five.
18. A man was born in 1898. What year was the man's fortieth birthday?
19. Each of the sides of a hexagon is three point two centimetres. What is its perimeter?
20. Look at the answer sheet. How many minutes does it take to get from the shopping centre to the cinema?

Test 6
Questions

"For this first set of questions you have five seconds to work out each answer and write it down."

1. Two numbers have a total of one thousand. One of the numbers is six hundred and ten. What is the other number?
2. Write the number that is four squared.
3. How many five pence pieces have the same value as three pounds?
4. How many degrees are there in half a turn?
5. Subtract seventeen from sixty.
6. The perimeter of a square is forty four centimetres. What is the length of one of its sides?

"For the next set of questions you have ten seconds to work out each answer and write it down."

7. The time is ten to four in the afternoon. Write this time as it would be shown on a twenty-four hour digital clock.
8. Look at the number sequence on your answer sheet. What is the next number?
9. How much change from five pounds would you get if you spent exactly twelve pence?
10. Find the difference between three hundred and fifty and five hundred and ten.
11. A TV programme starts at twenty five to seven and lasts for forty minutes. What time does the programme end?
12. On the answer sheet is part of a scale. What number is the arrow pointing to?
13. How many teams of nine people can be made from a group of fifty four people?
14. Jane is going on a two hundred and forty kilometre journey. She travels ninety kilometres and stops. How many kilometres has she still to go?
15. Circle the fraction that is equivalent to seventy per cent.

"For the next set of questions you have fifteen seconds to work out each answer and write it down."

16. A woman was born in 1898. What year was the woman's sixtieth birthday?
17. Which number is exactly half way between sixteen and thirty two?
18. Twenty five per cent of a number is thirteen. What is the number?
19. Circle the expression shown on your answer sheet that has an answer nearest to thirty.
20. Look at the pie chart on the answer sheet. Three hundred people were asked what their favourite car was. How many people said their favourite car was a Porsche?

Test 7
Questions

"For this first set of questions you have five seconds to work out each answer and write it down."

1. What is one third of twenty one?
2. Write the number thirty thousand and twenty seven in figures.
3. What is eight more than twenty seven?
4. Subtract thirty from one hundred and ten.
5. How many fifty pence coins have the same value as seven pounds?
6. How many metres are there in five and a half kilometres?

"For the next set of questions you have ten seconds to work out each answer and write it down."

7. Add five point four and three point six.
8. What is half of one thousand and forty?
9. A calculator costs fifteen pounds. In a sale the shop reduces all prices by ten per cent. How much does the calculator cost in the sale?
10. A TV programme lasts for fifty five minutes. It starts at seven thirty. What time does it end?
11. A girl buys a magazine costing two pounds forty. She pays with a ten pound note. How much change is she given?
12. On the answer sheet is part of a scale. What number is the arrow pointing to?
13. Imagine a triangular prism. How many of its faces are triangles?
14. The distance between Jo's house and the shop is one kilometre. Jo is walking from her house to the shop. She is exactly three quarters of the way there. How many metres has she still to walk?
15. How many degrees are there in three quarters of a turn?

"For the next set of questions you have fifteen seconds to work out each answer and write it down."

16. Which number is exactly half way between twelve and thirty four?
17. How many edges are there on a cube?
18. A football team scored five goals for every two they let in. They scored twenty five goals. How many did they let in?
19. One side of a square is ten point two centimetres. What is the perimeter of the square?
20. Circle the expression shown on your answer sheet that has an answer nearest to two hundred.

Test 8
Questions

"For this first set of questions you have five seconds to work out each answer and write it down."

1. What is eight multiplied by twenty five?
2. Subtract sixty from three hundred and ten.
3. Write the number seventeen thousand and four in figures.
4. How many centimetres are there in one point nine metres?
5. What is seventy five per cent as a decimal?
6. What number is four less than three thousand?

"For the next set of questions you have ten seconds to work out each answer and write it down."

7. An ice cream costs ninety nine pence and a lolly costs forty five pence. How much do they cost altogether?
8. The temperature yesterday was minus three degrees Celsius. The temperature today is two degrees colder. What is the temperature today?
9. Look at the answer sheet. In the equation, what is the value of x?
10. Multiply five by nine and add six.
11. Two numbers have a difference of twelve. One number is fifty. What could the other number be?
12. What is one third of twelve point nine?
13. Look at the answer sheet. Circle the number that is nearest to four kilograms.
14. Daniel slept for nine and a quarter hours without waking. He went to sleep at ten p.m. What time did he wake?
15. Look at the answer sheet. What is the median of the numbers?

"For the next set of questions you have fifteen seconds to work out each answer and write it down."

16. Look at the answer sheet. Draw a ring around the smallest of the five numbers.
15. A regular shape has a perimeter of seventy two centimetres. Each side is nine centimetres. What is the name of the shape?
18. I have fifty pence. My friend has six times that much. How much do we have altogether?
19. Which number is exactly half way between two thousand nine hundred and three thousand?
20. Look at the answer sheet. What is the size of angle P?

8

Test 9

Questions

"For this first set of questions you have five seconds to work out each answer and write it down."

1. Write the number that is ten squared.
2. Subtract forty five from eighty.
3. Two numbers have a total of two hundred. One of the numbers is twenty five. What is the other number?
4. How many fifty pence pieces have the same value as twelve pounds?
5. The time is quarter past eight in the evening. Write this time as it would be shown on a twenty-four hour digital clock.
6. The perimeter of a regular hexagon is forty two centimetres. What is the length of one of its sides?

"For the next set of questions you have ten seconds to work out each answer and write it down."

7. Find the difference between one hundred and seventy and two hundred and twenty.
8. Look at the number sequence on your answer sheet. What is the next number?
9. How much change from ten pounds would you get if you spent exactly six pounds and ninety five pence?
10. If I add nineteen to a number I get thirty two. What is the number?
11. A TV programme lasts for fifty minutes. It finishes at ten past four. What time does the programme start?
12. Look at your answer sheet. What is the area of the rectangle?
13. How many teams of six can be made from a group of fifty four people?
14. Calculate the total of one point six and one point seven.
15. Circle the decimal that is equivalent to ten per cent.

"For the next set of questions you have fifteen seconds to work out each answer and write it down."

16. Seventy five per cent of a number is thirty three. What is the number?
17. A square has an area of four centimetres squared. What is the length of one of its sides?
18. A woman has her twenty second birthday in the year two thousand and one. What year was the woman born?
19. Circle two fractions that are equivalent to one fifth.
20. Look at the pie chart on the answer sheet. Thirty people were asked what their favourite day of the week was. How many people said their favourite day was Saturday?

Test 10

Questions

"For this first set of questions you have five seconds to work out each answer and write it down."

1. What is the product of nine and four?
2. How many days are there in five weeks?
3. Write the number thirty thousand, four hundred in figures.
4. Reduce nine thousand by one.
5. How many millilitres are there in one point two five litres?
6. Write eight tenths as a fraction in its simplest form.

"For the next set of questions you have ten seconds to work out each answer and write it down."

7. A tin of beans costs forty five pence and a loaf of bread costs sixty eight pence. How much do the beans and bread cost altogether?
8. The temperature yesterday was minus four degrees Celsius. The temperature today is three degrees warmer. What is the temperature today?
9. What is one quarter of five point six?
10. Look at the answer sheet. In the equation, what is the value of q?
11. Which number is exactly half way between four and fourteen?
12. The time is twenty five past three in the afternoon. Write it as it would be shown on a twenty-four hour digital clock.
13. Look at the answer sheet. Circle the largest of the five numbers.
14. Lucy slept for ten and a half hours without waking. She went to sleep at nine p.m. What time did she wake?
15. Look at the answer sheet. What is the modal value of the set of numbers?

"For the next set of questions you have fifteen seconds to work out each answer and write it down."

16. There are three times as many children as adults at a funfair. There are exactly four hundred and forty people at the fair. How many are adults?
17. A regular shape has a perimeter of six point four centimetres. Each side is one point six centimetres. What is the name of the shape?
18. I have fifty two pence. My friend has four times that much. How much do we have altogether?
19. A car park costs thirty pence. Twenty cars visit the car park. How much money do they pay in total?
20. Look at the answer sheet. What is the size of angle R?

Test 11
Questions

"For this first set of questions you have five seconds to work out each answer and write it down."

1. What is twice fifty six?
2. Write the number thirteen thousand and five in figures.
3. How many sides do eight pentagons have in total?
4. What is eighteen more than twenty?
5. What is four point six multiplied by ten?
6. One tenth of the children in a class are boys. What percentage are boys?

"For the next set of questions you have ten seconds to work out each answer and write it down."

7. How many seconds are there in one and a quarter minutes?
8. One quarter of a number is three. What is the number?
9. What is half of five point two?
10. A snail crawls eleven centimetres. How much further does it have to crawl to reach one metre?
11. Add four and twenty nine and then divide by three.
12. On the answer sheet is part of a scale. What number is the arrow pointing to?
13. A shop has a sale. All items are twenty five per cent of their original prices. A video costs two pounds in the sale. What was its original price?
14. Dean walks eight miles every day. How far does he walk in a week?
15. What is the probability that the day after March 6th will be March 12th?

"For the next set of questions you have fifteen seconds to work out each answer and write it down."

16. Look at the answer sheet. Draw a ring around the number that is nearest to three.
17. Three tenths of a number is thirty. What is the number?
18. Which year is forty one years before the year two thousand and two?
19. Look at the answer sheet. What is the size of angle A?
20. Which of the expressions on your answer sheet has an answer nearest to forty?

Test 12
Questions

"For this first set of questions you have five seconds to work out each answer and write it down."

1. What is sixty divided by ten?
2. Two numbers have a total of one thousand. One of the numbers is four hundred and fifty. What is the other number?
3. The time is half past three in the afternoon. Write this time as it would be shown on a twenty-four hour digital clock.
4. How many ten pence pieces have the same value as five pounds?
5. How many weeks are there in four years?
6. What is the total number of degrees of the angles inside a triangle?

"For the next set of questions you have ten seconds to work out each answer and write it down."

7. Add thirteen and twenty two and then divide by seven.
8. Look at the number sequence on your answer sheet. What is the next number?
9. Two lengths add to make one metre. One of the lengths is twenty six centimetres. What is the other length?
10. Find the difference between one hundred and sixty and three hundred and ten.
11. A film lasts for one hour and twenty minutes. It starts at ten minutes to five. What time does it end?
12. On the answer sheet is part of a scale. What number is the arrow pointing to?
13. How much change from two pounds would you get if you spent exactly one pound thirty five pence?
14. How many teams of six can be made from a group of sixty six people?
15. Imagine a hexagonal prism. How many faces does it have?

"For the next set of questions you have fifteen seconds to work out each answer and write it down."

16. Add twenty one, forty eight and twelve.
17. Which number is exactly half way between fourteen and forty?
18. A man was born in 1942. How old was he in the year two thousand?
19. Each of the sides of a hexagon is one point two centimetres. What is its perimeter?
20. Look at the answer sheet. How many minutes does it take to get from the shopping centre to the cinema?

Test 1
Answer Sheet

5-second questions

1		4	ml
2		5	
3		6	

/6

10-second questions

7		12	6.8
8	°C	13	0.45 0.5 0.25 3.4 0.8
9	$x - 2.4 = 6.6$	14	
10		15	4 4 5 8 9
11	9.6		

/9

15-second questions

16	121 22 432 128 190	19	
17		20	G = ° 30° G
18	£		

/5

TOTAL /20

13

Test 2
Answer Sheet

5-second questions

1		4	
2	grams	5	
3		6	

10-second questions

7	
8	
9	£ ___ 65p, £5
10	
11	£ ___ £20

12		
13		
14		grams
15		3 : 1 40 children

15-second questions

16		3.2 cm
17		11.1
18		108

| 19 | | 2002 |
| 20 | | 17 34 99
$8\frac{1}{2}$ 49 $55\frac{1}{2}$ |

6

9

5

TOTAL 20

14

Test 3
Answer Sheet

5-second questions

1		4	grams
2		5	
3		6	

/6

10-second questions

7	£	12	17, …
8	°C	13	9.45 m 940 cm 9.5 m 955 cm 94 cm
9	$n - 63 = 37$	14	
10	86	15	$\frac{2}{10}$ $\frac{5}{10}$ $\frac{2}{10}$
11			

/9

15-second questions

16	3.8 4.002 2.99 2.9 4.02	19	
17		20	B = °
18	£		

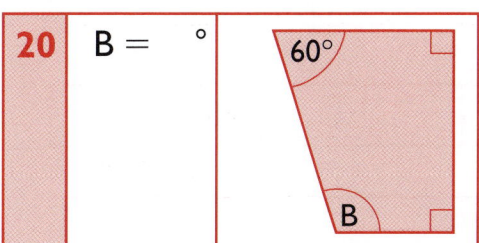

/5

TOTAL /20

Test 4
Answer Sheet

5-second questions

1	
2	
3	

4	ml
5	
6	

10-second questions

7	minutes
8	
9	$n - 28 = 42$
10	
11	

12	
13	0.9 9.0 9.1 0.09 90.0
14	
15	5 6 4 5 3 8

15-second questions

16	0.7 1.1 1.09 1.11 0.8
17	centimetres
18	

| 19 | 49 72 144 101 51 4 |
| 20 | bus station 12:52
shopping centre 12:56
swimming pool 13:11
cinema .... |

Test 5
Answer Sheet

5-second questions

1		4	
2		5	°
3		6	weeks

◯ 6

10-second questions

7		12	0.9 1
8		13	
9	centimetres	14	ml
10		15	5 : 2 / 15 goals
11	£		

◯ 9

15-second questions

16		34, 44	19		3.2 cm
17		22, 33, 45	20		bus station 15:42 / shopping centre 15:51 / swimming pool 16:16 / cinema 16:18
18		1898			

◯ 5

TOTAL ◯ 20

Test 6
Answer Sheet

5-second questions

1		4	
2		5	
3		6	cm

10-second questions

7	
8	29, 21, 13, 5, ...
9	£
10	
11	

12	
13	
14	km
15	$\frac{3}{4}$ $\frac{1}{7}$ $\frac{7}{10}$ $\frac{1}{70}$

15-second questions

16		1898
17		16, 32
18		

| 19 | 3.2×1.7 $\quad$ 32×1.7 0.32×17 $\quad$ 0.32×1.7 |

20 people 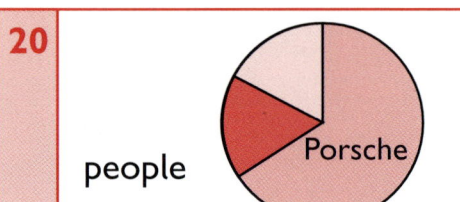 Porsche

Test 7
Answer Sheet

5-second questions

1	
2	
3	
4	
5	
6	metres

10-second questions

7	
8	
9	£ ___ £15
10	
11	£ ___ £2.40
12	(scale 300 to 400 with arrow)
13	
14	metres
15	°

15-second questions

16	12, 34
17	edges
18	5:2
19	10.2 cm
20	10.5 ÷ 20.3 105 ÷ 20.3 20.3 ÷ 1.05 203 ÷ 1.05

6
9
5
TOTAL 20

Test 8
Answer Sheet

5-second questions

1	
2	
3	

4	cm
5	
6	

10-second questions

7	£
8	°C
9	$x - 12 = 66$
10	
11	51

12	12.9
13	4.4 kg 410 g 4.5 kg 490 g 4300 g
14	
15	3 5 7 7 8

15-second questions

16	0.74 0.06 0.9 0.51 0.2
17	
18	£

| 19 | |
| 20 | P = ° 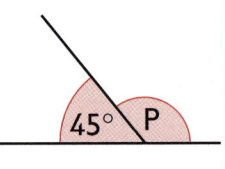 |

20

Test 9
Answer Sheet

5-second questions

1		4	
2		5	
3		6	cm

6

10-second questions

7	170, 220
8	100, 89, 78, 67, …
9	£
10	
11	

12	cm²	4.8 cm / 10 cm
13	
14	1.6, 1.7
15	11.0 0.1 10.0 0.01 1.0

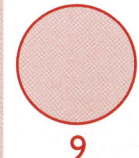
9

15-second questions

16	
17	Area = 4 cm²
18	2001

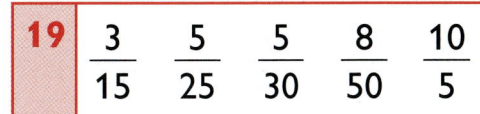

19 | $\frac{3}{15}$ | $\frac{5}{25}$ | $\frac{5}{30}$ | $\frac{8}{50}$ | $\frac{10}{5}$ |

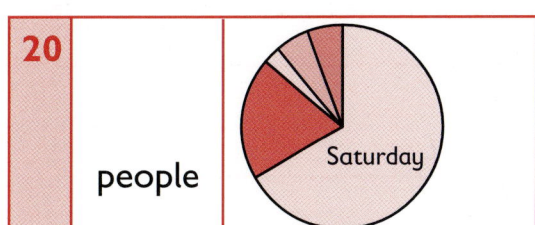

20 | people | Saturday

5

TOTAL
20

Test 10
Answer Sheet

5-second questions

1		4	
2	days	5	ml
3		6	

10-second questions

7	£	12	
8	°C	13	6.45 0.5489 0.699 6.4 6.5
9	5.6	14	
10	29 + q = 63	15	4 6 2 2 3 5 2
11	4, 14		

15-second questions

16	440	19	30p, 20
17	6.4 cm	20	R = ° 85° R
18	£		

6

9

5

TOTAL 20

Test 11
Answer Sheet

5-second questions

1		4	
2		5	
3		6	%

◯ 6

10-second questions

7	seconds
8	
9	
10	centimetres
11	

12	400 ↘600
13	£
14	miles
15	

◯ 9

15-second questions

16	3.0999 3.4 4.16 3.8 3.44
17	
18	

| 19 | A = | 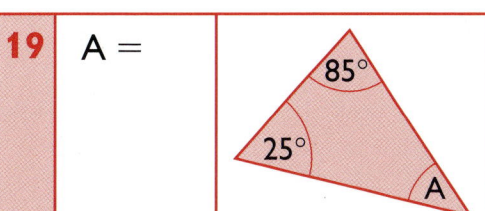 85° 25° A |
| 20 | 8.2 × 5.5   6.1 × 8.8   2.9 × 5.2   5.9 × 4.9 |

◯ 5

TOTAL ◯ 20

23

Test 12
Answer Sheet

5-second questions

1		4	
2		5	weeks
3		6	°

6

10-second questions

7	
8	3, 6, 12, 24, …
9	cm
10	160, 310
11	

12	 0.9 1
13	
14	
15	

9

15-second questions

16	21, 48, 12
17	14, 40
18	1942

| 19 | |
| 20 | bus station 13:42
shopping centre 13:49
swimming pool 14:08
cinema 14:12 |

5

TOTAL
20

24

Answers
Mental Tests

Test 1

1. 72
2. 12005
3. 70
4. 1200 ml
5. 2998
6. 0.9 or 0.90
7. 33
8. −3°C
9. 9 or 9.0
10. 7:10
11. 3.2
12. 8.2 or 5.4
13. 0.8
14. 6.30 a.m.
15. 5
16. 432
17. hexagon
18. £1.80
19. 3800
20. 150°

Notes:
- The median value is the number in the middle when the set is arranged in order.
- To find a number half way between two numbers, add them and divide by two.
- A regular shape has equal sides and equal angles.

Test 2

1. 89
2. 250 g
3. 180
4. 0.9 or 0.90
5. 5
6. 10
7. 6.2
8. 540
9. £4.35
10. $\frac{2}{5}$ or two fifths
11. £16
12. 5
13. 5
14. 250 g
15. 10
16. 12.8
17. 9.2
18. 27
19. 1989
20. 17

Notes:
- A vertex (plural: vertices) is the mathematical word for the corner of a shape.

Test 3

1. 21
2. 24
3. 11014
4. 1500 g
5. 0.3 or 0.30
6. 4996
7. £2.69
8. −6°C
9. 100
10. 8.6
11. 175
12. 33
13. 955 cm
14. 7.30 a.m.
15. $\frac{3}{10}$
16. 2.9
17. square
18. £4.50
19. 3500
20. 120°

Notes:
- The mean value can be found by adding the scores and dividing by the number of scores, in this case 3.
- The angles inside a four sided shape (a quadrilateral) total 360°.

Test 4

1. 44
2. 35
3. 10003
4. 250 ml
5. $\frac{7}{10}$
6. 240
7. 600
8. 150
9. 70
10. 27
11. 10
12. 22:15
13. 0.9
14. 9:55
15. 5
16. 1.09
17. 12 cm
18. semicircles
19. 49, 144, 4
20. 13:34

Notes:
- The mode is the number that occurs most often.
- Square numbers include 1, 4, 16, 25, 36, 49, 64, 81, 100.

Answers – Mental Tests

Test 5

1. 40016
2. 48
3. 6.7
4. 6
5. 60°
6. 104
7. 5
8. 2.6
9. 83 cm
10. 5.10
11. £6.50
12. 0.94
13. 1
14. 500 ml
15. 6
16. 39
17. 100
18. 1938
19. 19.2 cm
20. 27 minutes

Notes:
- A square is a special kind of rectangle with all equal sides.

Test 6

1. 390
2. 16
3. 60
4. 180°
5. 43
6. 11 cm
7. 15:50
8. −3
9. £4.88
10. 160
11. 7.15
12. 0.76
13. 6
14. 150 km
15. $\frac{7}{10}$
16. 1958
17. 24
18. 52
19. 32 × 1.7
20. 200

Notes:
- To square a number you multiply it by itself.
- Half a turn is equivalent to two right angles or 90° = total of 180°.

Test 7

1. 7
2. 30027
3. 35
4. 80
5. 14
6. 5500 m
7. 9 or 9.0
8. 520
9. £13.50
10. 8.25
11. £7.60
12. 350
13. 2
14. 250 m
15. 270°
16. 23
17. 12
18. 10
19. 40.8 cm
20. 203 ÷ 1.05

Notes:
- A prism is a shape with the same cross-section along its length, e.g. a Toblerone bar is a triangular prism.
- The edges of a 3D shape are the lines that join the corners and separate the faces.

Test 8

1. 200
2. 250
3. 17004
4. 190 cm
5. 0.75
6. 2996
7. £1.44
8. −5°C
9. 78
10. 51
11. 62 or 38
12. 4.3
13. 4300 g
14. 7.15 a.m.
15. 7
16. 0.06
17. octagon
18. £3.50
19. 2950
20. 135°

Notes:
- The median value is the number in the middle when the set is arranged in order. If two numbers occur in the middle, the median is exactly half way between the two numbers.

Answers – Mental Tests

Test 9

1. 100
2. 35
3. 175
4. 24
5. 20:15
6. 7 cm
7. 50
8. 56
9. £3.05
10. 13
11. 3.20
12. 48 cm²
13. 9
14. 3.3
15. 0.1
16. 44
17. 2 cm
18. 1979
19. $\frac{3}{15}, \frac{5}{25}$
20. 20

Notes:
- Children often confuse area and perimeter. Perimeter is the distance all the way around the edge of a shape. The area of a shape is the amount of surface inside the shape. For rectangles, this can be calculated by multiplying the length by the breadth.

Test 10

1. 36
2. 35
3. 30400
4. 8999
5. 1250 ml
6. $\frac{4}{5}$
7. £1.13
8. −1°C
9. 1.4
10. 34
11. 9
12. 15:25
13. 6.5
14. 7.30 a.m.
15. 2
16. 110
17. square
18. £2.60
19. £6
20. 95°

Notes:
- The modal value is the number that occurs most often.

Test 11

1. 112
2. 13005
3. 40
4. 38
5. 46
6. 10%
7. 75
8. 12
9. 2.6
10. 89 cm
11. 11
12. 580
13. £8
14. 56 miles
15. 0 or impossible
16. 3.0999
17. 100
18. 1961
19. 70°
20. 8.2 × 5.5

Notes:
- The angles inside a triangle have a total of 180°.
- The probability of an event that is impossible is zero.

Test 12

1. 6
2. 550
3. 15:30
4. 50
5. 208
6. 180°
7. 5
8. 48
9. 74 cm
10. 150
11. 6.10
12. 0.93
13. 65p
14. 11
15. 8
16. 81
17. 27
18. 58
19. 7.2 cm
20. 23

National Curriculum Levels

The Key Stage 2 National Tests are levelled according to the child's total score for the written Tests A and B and one mental test, similar to those in this book.

Mark	24 or below	25–51	52–79	80–100
Level	Level 1/2	Level 3	Level 4	Level 5

Scores for each mental test can be broadly broken down as follows:

Mark	0–4	5–10	11–15	16–20
Level	Level 1/2	Level 3	Level 4	Level 5

For practice in the written tests, look for the Key Stage 2 Maths books in this series. If your child needs more practice in any Maths topics, use the WH Smith Key Stage 2 Maths Revision Guide.

Practice Pages
5-Second Questions

MORE THAN/LESS THAN

What is:

1. twelve more than twenty?
2. nineteen more than fifteen?
3. seventeen less than fifty?
4. thirty two less than fifty?
5. four less than two thousand?
6. nine less than five hundred?

ADDING AND SUBTRACTING

Find the total of:

7. fourteen and twelve   eighteen and seventeen
8. twenty two and nine   thirty four and sixteen
9. Two numbers total one thousand. One of the numbers is three hundred and fifty. What is the other number?
10. Two numbers total one thousand. One of the numbers is seven hundred and twenty five. What is the other number?

Reduce:

11. sixteen by nine
12. one hundred and ten by twenty

Decrease:

13. fifty by eleven
14. forty by six

Practice Pages

MULTIPLYING AND DIVIDING

What is:

15 the product of six and five?

16 the product of nine and eight?

17 five multiplied by twenty?

18 seven point two multiplied by ten?

19 twelve point nine multiplied by ten?

20 forty two divided by six?

21 fifty four divided by nine?

22 sixty four divided by eight?

23 thirty five divided by ten?

24 one hundred and sixty divided by ten?

25 Write the number that is 8 squared.

26 Write the number that is 10 squared.

27 Write the number that is 20 squared.

28 How many sides do ten pentagons have in total?

29 How many sides do seven hexagons have in total?

30 How many sides do nine octagons have in total?

Practice Pages

DOUBLING AND HALVING

31 What is **double**:

eighteen? ☐   thirty two? ☐   fifty six? ☐

32 What is **twice**:

thirty nine? ☐   sixty eight? ☐   one point six? ☐

33 What is **half**:

fifty four? ☐   thirty eight? ☐   eighty eight? ☐

34 What is **half**:

sixty two? ☐   seventy four? ☐   ninety six? ☐

WRITING NUMBERS IN FIGURES

Write in figures the number:

35 three thousand and two ☐

36 five thousand and nine ☐

37 eight thousand and fourteen ☐

38 nine thousand and nineteen ☐

39 ten thousand and six ☐

40 eleven thousand and eighteen ☐

41 twenty thousand and five ☐

42 thirty thousand and twenty one ☐

43 forty thousand and thirty ☐

44 fifty thousand, four hundred ☐

31

Practice Pages

FRACTIONS, DECIMALS AND PERCENTAGES

What is:

45 one third of twenty four?

46 two thirds of thirty?

47 one quarter of sixty?

48 one fifth of fifteen?

49 one eighth of forty eight?

50 three quarters of twenty four?

51 What is three quarters as a decimal?

52 What is nine tenths as a decimal?

53 What is six hundredths as a decimal?

54 What is nought point two five as a fraction?

55 What is nought point three as a fraction?

56 What is nought point eight as a fraction in its simplest form?

57 Nine tenths of the children in a class are girls. What percentage are girls?

58 One fifth of the children in a class are boys. What percentage are boys?

59 One quarter of the children in a class are boys. What percentage are boys?

PROBABILITY

60 A bag contains five green cubes and one white cube. The probability of picking a green cube is five sixths. What is the probability of picking a white cube?

61 What is the probability of a coin landing on heads? Give your answer as a fraction.

62 What is the probability that the day after July 1st will be July 2nd?

MEASUREMENT AND MONEY

How many:

63 millilitres are there in four and a half litres?

64 grams are there in five point six kilograms?

65 grams are there in three quarters of a kilogram?

66 metres are there in one tenth of a kilometre?

67 ten pence coins have the same value as four pounds?

68 two pence pieces have the same value as two pounds?

69 five pence coins have the same value as four pounds?

70 twenty pence pieces have the same value as ten pounds?

71 months are there in four years?

72 days are there in six weeks?

73 minutes are there in six hours?

Practice Pages

MEASUREMENT AND MONEY

74 The time is quarter to three in the afternoon. Write this time as it would be shown on a twenty-four hour digital clock.

75 The time is quarter past five in the afternoon. Write this time as it would be shown on a twenty-four hour digital clock.

76 The time is ten to nine in the evening. Write this time as it would be shown on a twenty-four hour digital clock.

77 The perimeter of a square is 24 cm. What is the length of one of its sides?

78 The perimeter of a square is 36 cm. What is the length of one of its sides?

79 The perimeter of a regular pentagon is 40 cm. What is the length of one of its sides?

80 The perimeter of a regular hexagon is 42 cm. What is the length of one of its sides?

81 How many degrees are there in a triangle?

82 How many degrees is one of the angles in an equilateral triangle?

Practice Pages
10-Second Questions

CALCULATIONS

1. Add ten and fourteen and then divide by four.
2. Multiply seven by five and then subtract seven.
3. Add fifteen and nine and then divide by three.
4. Divide two hundred by four and then subtract seven.
5. How many teams of four people can be made from a group of thirty six people?
6. How many teams of nine people can be made from a group of fifty four people?
7. How many teams of eight people can be made from a group of thirty two people?
8. How many teams of four people can be made from a group of twenty eight people?

What is:

9. three point seven multiplied by ten?
10. eleven point six multiplied by ten?
11. thirty two point seven multiplied by one hundred?

READING SCALES

What numbers are the arrows pointing to?

12.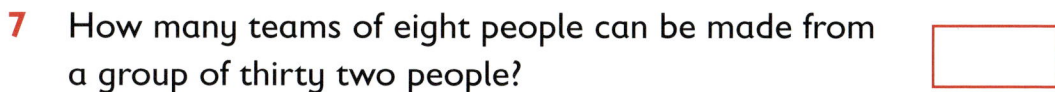

13.

Practice Pages

NEGATIVE NUMBERS

14 The temperature yesterday was minus seven degrees Celsius. The temperature today is three degrees warmer. What is the temperature today?

15 The temperature yesterday was minus two degrees Celsius. The temperature today is four degrees colder. What is the temperature today?

16 The temperature yesterday was five degrees Celsius. The temperature today is seven degrees colder. What is the temperature today?

NUMBER PATTERNS AND ALGEBRA

What is the next number in the sequence?

17 58, 53, 48, 43, ☐   37, 28, 19, 10, ☐

18 1, 3, 6, 10, ☐   22, 16, 10, 4, ☐

In the equation, what is the value of x?

19 $x + 17 = 38$ ☐ $x - 41 = 57$ ☐

20 $33 + x = 42$ ☐ $59 - x = 21$ ☐

Practice Pages

FRACTIONS, DECIMALS AND PERCENTAGES

21 One quarter of a number is five. What is the number? ☐

22 One third of a number is twelve. What is the number? ☐

23 One fifth of a number is five. What is the number? ☐

24 One ninth of a number is four. What is the number? ☐

25 One sixth of a number is seven. What is the number? ☐

26 A shop has a sale. Ten per cent is taken off all prices. What is the sale price of a book that was forty pounds? ☐

27 In a sale, items cost twenty five per cent of their original prices. A video costs £7 in the sale. What was its original price? ☐

28 Circle two equivalent fractions in each row.

$\frac{1}{2}$ $\frac{2}{3}$ $\frac{3}{4}$ $\frac{1}{4}$ $\frac{2}{6}$ $\frac{6}{8}$ $\frac{7}{10}$

$\frac{1}{3}$ $\frac{5}{6}$ $\frac{6}{9}$ $\frac{2}{4}$ $\frac{5}{7}$ $\frac{1}{8}$ $\frac{2}{3}$

$\frac{1}{10}$ $\frac{2}{3}$ $\frac{9}{12}$ $\frac{1}{6}$ $\frac{2}{5}$ $\frac{4}{8}$ $\frac{3}{4}$

29 What is 10% of:

380? ☐   490? ☐   34? ☐   127? ☐

Practice Pages

MEASUREMENT AND MONEY

30 A square has sides of 4 cm. What is its perimeter?

31 A square has sides of 9 cm. What is its perimeter?

32 A regular pentagon has sides of 4 cm. What is its perimeter?

33 A regular hexagon has sides of 8 cm. What is its perimeter?

34 A square has sides of 2 cm. What is its area?

35 A square has sides of 8 cm. What is its area?

36 A rectangle has sides of 5 cm and 4 cm. What is its area?

37 What is the area of this rectangle?   3.7 cm
                                            10 cm

38 I start with a five pound note. I spend one pound ninety five pence. How much have I now?

39 I start with a ten pound note. I spend three pounds seventy five pence. How much have I now?

40 A film started at twenty past seven. It finished at ten past eight. How many minutes did it last?

41 A film started at twenty to nine. It finished at ten o'clock. How many minutes did the film last?

Practice Pages
15-Second Questions

FRACTIONS, DECIMALS AND PERCENTAGES

1. Draw a ring around the number that is nearest to three.

   3.2   3.46   3.9   3.19   3.7

2. Draw a ring around the number that is nearest to four.

   4.11   4.46   4.089   3.8   4.39

3. Seventy five per cent of a number is nine. What is the number?

4. Seventy five per cent of a number is thirty three. What is the number?

5. Thirty per cent of a number is eighteen. What is the number?

6. One fifth of a number is twenty five. What is the number?

CALCULATIONS OF TIME

7. A woman was born in 1897. Which birthday did she have in 1909?

8. Which year is twenty three years before the year two thousand and two?

9. A man was born in 1887. What year was the man's forty ninth birthday?

Practice Pages

NUMBER KNOWLEDGE

10 Which number is exactly half way between two thousand five hundred and three thousand?

11 Which number is exactly half way between three thousand and six thousand?

12 Which number is exactly half way between twenty two and fifty four?

13 Which number is exactly half way between fourteen and forty two?

MONEY PROBLEMS

14 I went to the shop with five pounds. I spent forty five pence and then sixty seven pence. How much did I have left?

15 I went to the shop with ten pounds. I spent eighty pence and then two pounds and fifteen pence. How much did I have left?

16 A car park costs forty pence. Twenty cars visit the car park. How much money do they pay in total?

17 A car park costs sixty pence. Eleven cars visit the car park. How much money do they pay in total?

18 I have eighty pence. My friend has three times that much. How much do we have altogether?

Practice Pages

SHAPE AND MEASUREMENT

19 What is the size of angle C?

20 What is the size of angle A?

21 What is the size of angle B?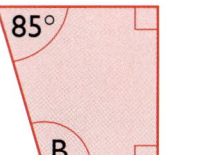

22 How many faces does a triangular prism have?

23 How many edges does a cube have?

24 How many vertices does a square pyramid have?

DATA HANDLING

25 Look at the pie chart. One hundred and eighty people were asked what their favourite food was. How many people said their favourite food was chips?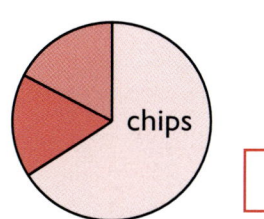

26 Here are some start and finish times of TV programmes. How long did the travel programme last?

	Start	Finish
Documentary	14:25	15:20
Travel	16:33	17:06
Wildlife	19:36	20:27

Answers
Practice Pages

5-second questions

1. 32
2. 34
3. 33
4. 18
5. 1996
6. 491

7. 26, 35
8. 31, 50
9. 650
10. 275
11. 7
12. 90
13. 39
14. 34

15. 30
16. 72
17. 100
18. 72
19. 129
20. 7
21. 6
22. 8
23. 3.5
24. 16
25. 64
26. 100
27. 400
28. 50
29. 42
30. 72

31. 36, 64, 112
32. 78, 136, 3.2
33. 27, 19, 44
34. 31, 37, 48

35. 3002
36. 5009
37. 8014
38. 9019
39. 10006
40. 11018
41. 20005
42. 30021
43. 40030
44. 50400

45. 8
46. 20
47. 15
48. 3
49. 6
50. 18
51. 0.75
52. 0.9
53. 0.06
54. $\frac{1}{4}$
55. $\frac{3}{10}$
56. $\frac{4}{5}$
57. 90%
58. 20%
59. 25%

60. $\frac{1}{6}$
61. $\frac{1}{2}$
62. certain or 1

63. 4500 ml
64. 5600 g
65. 750 g
66. 100 m
67. 40
68. 100
69. 80
70. 50
71. 48
72. 42
73. 360

74. 14:45
75. 17:15
76. 20:50
77. 6 cm
78. 9 cm
79. 8 cm
80. 7 cm
81. 180°
82. 60°

Answers – Practice Pages

10-second questions

1. 6
2. 28
3. 8
4. 43
5. 9
6. 6
7. 4
8. 7
9. 37
10. 116
11. 3270

12. 1300, 6.78
13. 940, 0.11

14. −4°C
15. −6°C
16. −2°C

17. 38, 1
18. 15, −2
19. 21, 98
20. 9, 38

21. 20
22. 36
23. 25
24. 36
25. 42
26. £36
27. £28
28. $\frac{3}{4}, \frac{6}{8}$
    $\frac{6}{9}, \frac{2}{3}$
    $\frac{9}{12}, \frac{3}{4}$
29. 38, 49, 3.4, 12.7

30. 16 cm
31. 36 cm
32. 20 cm
33. 48 cm
34. 4 cm²
35. 64 cm²
36. 20 cm²
37. 37 cm²
38. £3.05
39. £6.25
40. 50 minutes
41. 80 minutes

Answers – Practice Pages

15-second questions

1. 3.19
2. 4.089
3. 12
4. 44
5. 60
6. 125

7. 12th
8. 1979
9. 1936

10. 2750
11. 4500
12. 38
13. 28

14. £3.88
15. £7.05
16. £8
17. £6.60
18. £3.20

19. 105°
20. 90°
21. 95°
22. 5
23. 12
24. 5

25. 120
26. 33 minutes